SRI LANKA TRAVEL GUIDE 2024

Experience Must-see Attractions, Natural Wonders, Where to Stay, Things to do and what to Eat in the Stunning Island

Emmaline Gill

All rights reserved. No part of this publication may be reproduced, distributed, or transmitted in any form or by any means, including
photocopying, recording, or other electronic or mechanical methods, without the prior written permission of the publisher, except in the case of brief quotations embodied in critical reviews and certain other noncommercial uses permitted by copyright law.

Copyright © Emmaline Gill, 2024.

Table of Contents

CHAPTER 1: PLANNING YOUR TRIP TO SRI LANKA 4
- The Serendipity of Sri Lanka 4
- 1.1 Best Time to Visit 6
- 1.2 Budgeting Your Trip 8
- 1.3 Visa and Travel Documents 16
- 1.4 Health and Safety Tips 19

CHAPTER 2: MUST-SEE ATTRACTIONS AND LANDMARKS 22
- 2.1 Historical Sites 22
- 2.2 Natural Wonders 25
- 2.3 UNESCO World Heritage Sites 30

CHAPTER 3: ACCOMMODATION OPTIONS 34
- 3.1 Hotels and Resorts 34
- 3.2 Guest Houses and B&Bs 39
- 3.3 Eco-Lodges and Camping 42

CHAPTER 4: DINING AND CUISINE 54
- 4.1 Authentic Sri Lankan Culinary Delights 54
- 4.2 Street Food and Snacks 57

CHAPTER 5: THINGS TO DO AND OUTDOOR ACTIVITIES 62
- 5.1 Beach Activities 62
- 5.2 Wildlife and Nature Tours 69
- 5.3 Adventure Sports 72

CHAPTER 6: ART, CULTURE, AND ENTERTAINMENT 76
- 6.1 Traditional Music and Dance 76
- 6.2 Art Galleries and Museums 78
- 6.3 Festivals and Events 83

CHAPTER 7: 7-DAY ITINERARY 88

7.1 Day 1-3: Colombo and Surroundings 88
Day 1: Colombo 88
Day 2: Kandy 89
Day 3: Nuwara Eliya 91
Day 4: Kandy 93
Day 5: The Hill Country 95

7.3 Day 6-7: Galle and the South Coast 97
Day 6: Galle Fort and Unawatuna 97
Day 7: Mirissa and Weligama 98

CHAPTER 8: PRACTICAL INFORMATION AND TIPS 100

8.1 Local Customs and Etiquette 100
8.2 Transportation Tips 102
8.3 Useful Phrases in Sinhala 104

CONCLUSION 108

9.1 Final Thoughts 108

Chapter 1: Planning Your Trip to Sri Lanka

The Serendipity of Sri Lanka

Stepping off the plane in 2024, I was immediately embraced by Sri Lanka's warm tropical climate, sparking my sense of adventure for the Journey ahead. This book commemorates that remarkable voyage - a thoughtful guide to help you navigate the captivating landscapes of this island nation, just as I did.

Every moment presented a discovery, from Colombo's lively streets, fragranced by mouthwatering local cuisine, to Bentota's peaceful shores promising tranquil reprieve. Anuradhapura's ancient ruins whispered stories of past eras, while Nuwara Eliya's lush greenery was a refreshing contrast to the golden sandy coastlines.

This is not merely a recounting of my travels but a sincere effort to transport you to Sri Lanka - to feel the sand between your toes, hear the gentle rustle of tea plantation leaves, and experience the tangy flavors of authentic Sri Lankan dishes. It is a guide, a companion, and a glimpse into my reflections as I uncover Sri Lanka's beauty and charm, one remarkable experience at a time.

So, let us embark on this Journey together. Because travel is not just about the destination - it's the adventures we have, the connections we make, and the narratives we create. And with its rich cultural heritage and breathtaking scenery, Sri Lanka promises a tale you'll be eager to tell.

1.1 Best Time to Visit

Sri Lanka is an enticing destination throughout the year, yet the optimal time for your visit hinges on the region you wish to explore. The island experiences two distinct monsoon seasons, influencing various areas simultaneously. Here's an overview of the weather patterns and the most favorable months for exploration in each region:

Southwest Coast and Hill Country:

The southwest monsoon, gracing the western, southern, and central parts of Sri Lanka from May to September, brings a cascade of rain. However, the pinnacle of delight for these regions occurs from December to March, offering dry, sunlit days with pleasant temperatures. This period is ideal for whale watching and reveling in water sports along the southern coast. Despite the allure, it's also the peak season, marked by crowds and higher expenses. Planning, booking accommodations, and transportation or opting for less-traveled destinations might be prudent. Noteworthy attractions in this region encompass Colombo, Galle, Kandy, Nuwara Eliya, and Yala National Park.

Northeast Coast:

Conversely, the northeast monsoon ushers rain for the eastern and northern parts of Sri Lanka from November to February. The prime period for exploration unfolds from April to September, characterized by dry, hot weather conducive to swimming and surfing on the pristine beaches. This is the opportune time to visit ancient cities like Anuradhapura, Polonnaruwa, and Sigiriya and partake in cultural festivals such as Vesak and Kandy Esala Perahera. However, it is also the hottest and most humid stretch of the year, necessitating precautions against the midday sun. Key highlights of this region include Trincomalee, Arugam Bay, Jaffna, and Wilpattu National Park.

Naturally, these are broad guidelines, subject to the erratic nature of weather. Rain or sunshine may surprise you anytime, emphasizing the importance of checking the forecast before your Journey and packing accordingly. Sri Lanka promises a trove of natural beauty, cultural heritage, wildlife, and cuisine, ensuring a memorable experience whenever you choose to visit.

1.2 Budgeting Your Trip

Sri Lanka is a captivating destination, offering many experiences, from exploring ancient temples and embarking on wildlife safaris to enjoying pristine beaches and lush tea plantations. The question arises: what is the cost associated with traveling in Sri Lanka in 2024, and how can one meticulously plan their budget? The positive aspect is that Sri Lanka remains a relatively affordable country to visit, especially compared to neighboring nations in Asia. However, it's crucial to note the recent upward trend in prices, making it essential to conduct thorough research and plan to optimize your expenses.

This segment aims to provide practical tips and guidance on budgeting for your Sri Lankan journey, considering diverse travel styles and preferences. Examples of typical costs for accommodation, transportation, food, and entertainment will be presented, accompanied by suggestions on saving money and avoiding potential scams. Whether you are a budget-conscious backpacker, a mid-range traveler seeking comfort and convenience, or a luxury enthusiast ready to indulge, our comprehensive guide is designed to cater to your needs.

How Much Does It Cost to Travel in Sri Lanka?

The response to this inquiry hinges on various factors, including your travel preferences, itinerary, the season of your visit, and individual choices. Nonetheless, to offer a broad overview, here are approximate daily budgets for different types of travelers in Sri Lanka in 2024:

- **Backpacker:** $20-$30 per day
- **Mid-range:** $50-$80 per day
- **Luxury:** $100-$200 per day

These are rough estimates, and your actual expenses may vary depending on the decisions you make during your Journey. Traveling during the peak season (December to March) could result in higher costs for accommodation and flights. Conversely, the low season (May to September) might present great deals and discount opportunities.

It's important to note that these budgets exclude essential expenses like visa fees, flights, travel insurance, and vaccinations. These costs should be factored in before finalizing your travel plans. A more detailed discussion of these expenses will be provided later in this section.

How to Budget for Accommodation in Sri Lanka

Lodging is a significant expense when journeying through Sri Lanka, yet it offers various choices to cater to every preference and budget. Ranging from modest hostels and guesthouses to opulent resorts and villas, the accommodation options are extensive, ensuring there's something to align with your needs and expectations.

Here are some examples illustrating the typical costs of accommodation in Sri Lanka for 2024, based on average prices sourced from Booking.com:

- Hostel dorm: $5-$10 per night
- Guesthouse or homestay: $10-$20 per night
- Budget hotel: $20-$40 per night
- Mid-range hotel: $40-$80 per night
- Luxury hotel or resort: $80-$200 per night

The price range varies significantly based on the type and quality of accommodation you select. Therefore, researching and comparing different options before finalizing your stay is crucial.

Consider the following money-saving tips to enhance your lodging experience:

- **Book in advance:** Particularly crucial during peak seasons, bookings can secure your spot and potentially offer better rates. Utilize platforms like Booking.com or Agoda to compare options and read reviews.

- **Use discount codes or coupons:** Seek discount codes or coupons for potential savings. Websites like Coupon Lanka or PromoLk may have offers suitable for your travel dates and destinations.

- **Negotiate the price:** When booking directly with the accommodation, negotiating the price might be possible, especially for longer stays or during low seasons. Politeness is key, and while some discounts may be available, expecting substantial bargains may not always be realistic.

- **Stay in less touristy areas:** Opting for less popular or rural areas can yield cost savings and a more authentic experience. Staying in homestays or guesthouses in small villages allows for cultural immersion and scenic enjoyment. However, be prepared for potential trade-offs in comfort and convenience, and factor in transportation costs and time to reach main attractions.

How to Budget for Transportation in Sri Lanka

Transportation constitutes a significant aspect of the budget when exploring Sri Lanka, but fortunately, it presents a myriad of options catering to diverse preferences and financial plans. From bustling public buses and scenic trains to the iconic tuk-tuks and private taxis, there's a mode of transportation suited to every traveler's needs.

Here are exemplifications of typical transportation costs in Sri Lanka for 2024, derived from average prices on Rome2rio:

- Bus: $0.10-$0.50 per km
- Train: $0.20-$1.00 per km
- Tuk-tuk: $0.30-$0.60 USD per km
- Taxi: $0.50-$1.00 USD per km
- Private driver: $40-$80 per day

The substantial variation in prices underscores the importance of thorough research and comparison before securing your mode of transport.

Consider the following tips to optimize your budget and find the most suitable deals:

- **Use public transportation:** Embrace the authenticity and affordability of public buses and trains, offering a chance to mingle with locals and savor the scenery. Websites like Bus Booking or Train Ticket facilitate online ticket purchases, or you can acquire them at stations or on board.

- **Hire a tuk-tuk:** Navigate Sri Lanka conveniently and enjoyably via tuk-tuks, which are particularly useful in reaching areas inaccessible by bus or train. Apps like PickMe or Uber streamline the process but exercise caution regarding noise, bumps, and safety. Agree on pricing and destination beforehand, using a meter or map to avoid overcharges.

- **Rent a car or motorbike:** Unlock the freedom to explore Sri Lanka at your own pace by renting a car or motorbike. While it offers flexibility, be mindful of potential expenses, risks, and stresses associated with traffic and roads. Websites like Rentalcars.com or BikesBooking.com facilitate online bookings, or you can opt for local agencies or hotel rentals. Ensure the vehicle's condition and documents are in order, possess a valid license, and secure an international driving permit.

How to Budget for Food in Sri Lanka

Exploring Sri Lanka is a culinary delight, with a rich array of delectable dishes such as spicy curries, fragrant rice, fresh seafood, and tropical fruits. The question arises: What is the cost of dining in Sri Lanka in 2024, and how can you adeptly plan your budget?

The encouraging news is that food is inexpensive in Sri Lanka, particularly when indulging in local cuisine at street stalls, markets, or neighborhood eateries. Prices can fluctuate based on the chosen type and food quality, with some Western or international dishes leaning towards the pricier side.

Here are examples delineating typical food costs in Sri Lanka for 2024, derived from average prices on [Numbeo]:

- Street food or snack: $0.50-$1.00
- Local meal at a cheap restaurant: $1.00-$3.00
- Western or international meal at a mid-range restaurant: $5.00-$10.00
- Fine dining at a high-end restaurant: $10.00-$20.00

The substantial price disparities underscore the importance of research and comparison before embarking on your culinary Journey.

Consider these tips to optimize your budget and discover the best dining deals:

Eat local: Immerse yourself in the authentic flavors of Sri Lanka by indulging in local dishes like hoppers, kottu, dal, and pol sambol. Local food gems can be found at street stalls, markets, or humble local restaurants, offering a satisfying meal for less than $3. Exercise caution regarding hygiene and food safety standards.

1.3 Visa and Travel Documents

Sri Lanka, nestled in the Indian Ocean, is a captivating island nation boasting a rich culture, diverse wildlife, and breathtaking landscapes. If you're gearing up to visit this remarkable country, securing the necessary visa and organizing travel documents is a crucial step in your Journey.

Various types of visas cater to different purposes and durations of stay in Sri Lanka. The widely used Electronic Travel Authorization (ETA) is an online visa granting entry for tourism, transit, or business activities. ETA applications can be submitted through the official website or a registered travel agent, offering a validity of 30 days, extendable up to six months.

To initiate an ETA application, ensure you possess a passport valid for at least six months beyond your intended stay, a confirmed return ticket, proof of ample funds, a recent photograph (if applying online), and relevant documents supporting your travel purpose. The ETA fee varies by nationality, ranging from $0 to $35 for tourists and $40 for business travelers, payable online via credit or debit card or in cash at the airport upon arrival.

Alternatively, a visa-on-arrival option is available for citizens of 21 countries, including China, India, Japan, and Russia. Like the ETA, the visa on arrival grants a 30-day stay, extendable up to six months. However, the associated fee is higher, amounting to $40 for tourists and $50 for business travelers. The application involves completing a form and submitting requisite documents at the visa counter upon arrival.

For stays exceeding six months or for non-tourism purposes like employment, education, or journalism, a long-term visa from the nearest Sri Lankan embassy or consulate is necessary. The requirements and fees for long-term visas vary based on the type and category.

Beyond the visa, essential travel documents include:

- Your passport has at least two blank pages and six months of validity.
- A copy of your ETA approval notice or visa-on-arrival receipt.
- A printout of your return or onward flight ticket.
- Proof of accommodation, such as a hotel reservation or a host letter.
- Proof of vaccination if arriving from a yellow fever or polio-risk country.

- A travel insurance policy covering medical expenses, repatriation, and personal liability (recommended for safety).

By diligently preparing your visa and travel documents, you pave the way for a seamless and stress-free entry into Sri Lanka, allowing you to immerse yourself in the wonders of this enchanting island paradise. Whether seeking adventure, culture, nature, or relaxation, Sri Lanka promises an unforgettable experience marked by charm and hospitality.

1.4 Health and Safety Tips

Sri Lanka is a captivating and diverse destination, offering many attractions and experiences for travelers. However, like any locale, it presents health and safety considerations that necessitate awareness and preparation. Here are insightful tips to ensure your well-being during your vacation in Sri Lanka.

Secure your visa and vaccinations in advance: Obtain your visa, a prerequisite for entry into Sri Lanka, online three days before or after arrival. Opting for an online application proves cost-effective and expeditious. Consult your doctor or a travel clinic regarding recommended vaccinations, including hepatitis A, typhoid, tetanus, and rabies. Some vaccines require multiple doses, so plan to administer them at least four weeks before your departure.

Exercise caution with tap water: The tap water in Sri Lanka isn't potable, potentially harboring bacteria, parasites, or chemicals leading to illnesses. Rely on bottled water or employ a water purifier or filter before consumption. Refrain from using tap water to brush teeth, and exercise caution with ice cubes unless they are certain of their purification process.

Savor local cuisine with care: Sri Lankan gastronomy, influenced by India, China, and other regions, offers a delectable array of dishes. Enjoy local delicacies like rice, curry, hoppers, kottu, and dosas. However, be mindful of food hygiene and freshness, especially if you have a sensitive stomach. Avoid consuming raw or undercooked meat, seafood, eggs, or dairy, as they may harbor bacteria or parasites. Exercise caution with fruits or vegetables that haven't been peeled or washed with purified water. Opt for busy and popular local eateries to increase the likelihood of receiving fresh and safe food.

Respect local culture and religion: Sri Lanka boasts a multicultural and multi-religious landscape, predominantly Buddhist but also home to Hindus, Muslims, and Christians. Display respect for local customs and beliefs, dressing modestly when visiting religious sites. Refrain from photographing Buddha statues or paintings, as it's considered disrespectful. Avoid touching or turning your back to Buddha images, and refrain from posing with them. If donating or offering a flower, use your right or both hands, as the left hand is considered unclean.

Stay informed about the political situation: Sri Lanka, having recently emerged from civil conflict and economic challenges, is still undergoing political and social transformations. Stay vigilant regarding the current situation, avoiding areas prone to protests, demonstrations, or strikes that may disrupt services. Follow the guidance of local authorities, register with your embassy or consulate, and stay updated with the latest travel advice from your government or the FCDO.

Chapter 2: Must-See Attractions and Landmarks

2.1 Historical Sites

Sri Lanka is a nation steeped in a rich tapestry of history and culture, boasting numerous historical sites that offer a glimpse into its captivating past. Whether your interests lie in ancient kingdoms, colonial architecture, or religious monuments, the country presents many options to cater to your tastes. Here are some of the most renowned historical sites in Sri Lanka that should be on your must-visit list.

Sigiriya Rock Fortress: A UNESCO World Heritage Site and an iconic landmark, the Sigiriya Rock Fortress towers 200 meters above the plains. Once the royal palace of King Kasyapa in the 5th century, it now allows visitors to climb to its summit, offering breathtaking views of the surroundings and remnants of the palace, gardens, and frescoes. A nearby attraction is Pidurangala Rock, providing an excellent perspective of Sigiriya Rock. The entrance fee for Sigiriya Rock Fortress is 4,500 LKR ($22) for foreigners and welcomes visitors from 7 am to

5 pm. Transportation options include buses, taxis, or tuk-tuks from Dambulla, approximately 25 km away.

Dambulla Cave Temple: Another UNESCO World Heritage Site, the Dambulla Cave Temple is a remarkable complex comprising five caves adorned with over 150 statues and paintings of Buddha dating back to the 1st century BC. Perched on a hill, it offers scenic views of the surrounding countryside. The entrance fee for Dambulla Cave Temple is 1,500 LKR ($7.5) for foreigners, and visiting hours are from 7 am to 7 pm. Accessible by bus, taxi, or tuk-tuk from Sigiriya, which is around 25 km away.

Scan the QR code or Click on the Link for Map Directions

Temple of the Tooth: Situated in the city of Kandy, the Temple of the Tooth is a UNESCO World Heritage Site and holds immense significance for Buddhists. Housing a relic believed to be Buddha's tooth, the Temple showcases beautiful Sri Lankan architecture. Pilgrims and tourists flock to witness daily ceremonies and rituals. Surrounding attractions include Kandy Lake, the Royal Palace, and the National Museum. The Temple of the

Tooth entrance fee is 1,500 LKR ($7.5) for foreigners, and it opens from 5:30 am to 8 pm. Accessible by train, bus, or taxi from Colombo, approximately 120 km away.

These historical sites are just a glimpse of what Sri Lanka offers. The country's diversity and beauty, whether you're a history buff, nature lover, or culture enthusiast, promise a truly memorable experience. Don't hesitate to book your trip to Sri Lanka today and delve into the wonders of its remarkable historical sites. Your Journey awaits!

2.2 Natural Wonders

Sri Lanka stands as a treasure trove of natural marvels, showcasing nature's captivating beauty and diversity across its landscapes. From verdant rainforests and mist-covered mountains to exotic wildlife and unspoiled beaches, Sri Lanka caters to the heart's desires of every nature enthusiast. In this section, we will delve into some of the most awe-inspiring natural wonders Sri Lanka offers, beckoning you to explore these marvels in the year 2024.

Horton Plains National Park:

Nestled in the central highlands of Sri Lanka, Horton Plains National Park is a UNESCO World Heritage Site, encompassing 3,160 hectares. This sanctuary is a haven for a myriad of flora and fauna, including endemic and endangered species. Renowned for its picturesque landscapes, the park features expansive grasslands, ethereal cloud forests, enchanting waterfalls, and rugged rocky outcrops. World's End stands out among its attractions—a sheer cliff plunging 870 meters to the valley below, providing a breathtaking panoramic vista. Another gem within the park is Baker's Falls, a 20-

meter-high cascade over a series of rocks. Horton Plains is an ideal destination for hiking, birdwatching, and camping activities.

To explore Horton Plains National Park, an entrance ticket is required, obtainable at the park gate. The cost is 3,500 LKR (18 USD) for foreign visitors and 60 LKR (0.3 USD) for locals. The park operates daily from 6:00 am to 6:00 pm, with the optimal time for a visit being early morning when visibility is optimal and the weather is delightful. Access to the park is possible by car, bus, or train from Nuwara Eliya, which is approximately 32 km away. Alternatively, guided tours from Nuwara Eliya or Colombo are available, encompassing transportation, entrance fees, and the expertise of a guide. Embark on a journey to Horton Plains National Park and immerse yourself in the wonders of Sri Lanka's natural splendor.
Contact number: +94 522 222 646
Website:

Sinharaja Rainforest

The Sinharaja Rainforest, nestled in southwest Sri Lanka, is a UNESCO World Heritage Site, sprawling across 8,864 hectares. It stands as the last remaining lowland rainforest in the country, boasting a distinction as one of the most biodiverse places globally. This lush expanse harbors over 50% of Sri Lanka's endemic species, including mammals, birds, reptiles, amphibians, butterflies, and a staggering array of over 1,000 plant species. The forest serves as a sanctuary for rare and iconic creatures like the Sri Lankan leopard, the purple-faced langur, the red-faced malkoha, and the blue magpie. Beyond its natural wonders, the Sinharaja Rainforest is steeped in cultural and historical significance, featuring ancient temples, caves, and legends.

To explore the Sinharaja Rainforest, an entrance ticket must be acquired at the forest office, priced at 2,000 LKR (10 USD) for foreign visitors and 40 LKR (0.2 USD) for locals. Hiring a guide is also essential, with a typical charge of around 1,000 LKR (5 USD) per group. The forest welcomes visitors daily from 6:30 am to 6:00 pm, with the optimal time for a visit being from January to April when rainfall is minimal and trails are dry.

Access to the forest is facilitated by car, bus, or train from Colombo, which is approximately 160 km away. For a hassle-free experience, guided tours from Colombo or Galle are available, encompassing transportation, entrance fees, a guide, and

accommodation. Immerse yourself in the wonders of the Sinharaja Rainforest, a testament to Sri Lanka's natural splendor and diversity.
Contact number: +94 452 222 714
Website:

Yala National Park

Yala National Park, the second-largest and most frequented national park in Sri Lanka, spans an expansive 97,878 hectares in the country's southeastern part. The park is partitioned into five blocks, with only two accessible to the public. Renowned for its diverse wildlife, Yala is home to endangered species such as the Sri Lankan elephant and sloth bear. However, its crown jewel is the Sri Lankan leopard, boasting the highest density of these majestic creatures globally. The park features varied habitats, including scrub jungles, grasslands, wetlands, and beaches, creating an ideal environment for a rich array of wildlife.

For those eager to explore Yala National Park, acquiring an entrance ticket at the park gate is a prerequisite, priced at 4,000 LKR (20 USD) for foreigners and 80 LKR (0.4 USD) for locals. Additionally, securing a jeep and driver is essential, with an average cost of around 5,000 LKR (25 USD) per group. The park welcomes visitors daily from 6:00 am to 6:00 pm, with the optimal time for a visit falling between February and July when water levels recede, enhancing wildlife visibility.

Access to the park is facilitated by car, bus, or train from Colombo, approximately 300 km away. Alternatively, guided tours from Colombo or Galle offer a comprehensive experience, covering transportation, entrance fees, jeep, driver, and accommodation. Immerse yourself in the wonders of Yala National Park, where the untamed beauty of Sri Lanka's wildlife awaits.
Contact number: +94 472 222 714
Website:

2.3 UNESCO World Heritage Sites

Sri Lanka is rich in cultural and natural heritage, with eight sites inscribed on the UNESCO World Heritage List. These sites represent the diversity and history of this island nation, from ancient cities and temples to lush forests and mountains. If you are looking for some of the most remarkable and memorable places to visit in Sri Lanka, you should not miss these UNESCO World Heritage Sites.

Scan the QR code or Click on the link for map directions.

Sigiriya Ancient City, famously known as the Lion Rock, derives its name from the colossal lion-shaped gateway guiding visitors to the summit of the rock fortress. Constructed in the 5th century CE by King Kashyapa, who chose it as his royal residence and capital, Sigiriya boasts remarkable frescoes, meticulously landscaped gardens, intricate waterworks, and formidable fortifications.

Sigiriya offers breathtaking panoramic views of the surrounding landscape, an exemplary illustration of ancient urban planning and engineering prowess. The site welcomes visitors daily from 6:30 am to 5:30 pm, with an entrance fee of 4,500 LKR (approximately 22 USD) for foreigners. Accessible from nearby towns like Dambulla, Habarana, or Kandy, Sigiriya can be reached by bus, taxi, or the iconic tuk-tuk.

Scan the QR code or Click on the link for map directions.

The Golden Temple of Dambulla, also recognized as the Dambulla Cave Temple, encompasses five caves adorned with more than 150 statues and paintings depicting Buddha and various deities. Dating back to the 1st century BCE, the Temple has undergone extensive expansion and renovation by successive kings and monks. Functioning as a sacred pilgrimage site for Buddhists, the Temple stands as a testament to the rich art and architecture of Sri Lanka. Open every day from 6:00 am to 7:15 pm, the entrance fee for foreigners is 1,500 LKR (approximately 7 USD). Accessible from nearby towns like Dambulla, Sigiriya, or Kandy, the Temple can be reached by bus, taxi, or the traditional tuk-tuk.

Scan the QR code or Click on the link for map directions.

The Central Highlands of Sri Lanka encompass three protected areas: Peak Wilderness Protected Area, Horton Plains National Park, and Knuckles Conservation Forest, covering a vast expanse of 56,844 hectares filled with montane and submontane forests, grasslands, wetlands, and cascading waterfalls. This region is a haven for diverse endemic flora and fauna, playing host to threatened species like the Sri Lankan leopard, the purple-faced langur, and the Horton Plains slender loris. Beyond its ecological significance, the site holds cultural and spiritual importance, housing the sacred mountain of Sri Pada, also known as Adam's Peak.

This revered location attracts followers from various faiths, including Buddhists, Hindus, Christians, and Muslims, who believe it to be the site of Buddha's, Shiva's, Adam's, or St. Thomas's footprint. Accessible year-round, the optimal period to visit is from December to April when the weather is dry and skies

32

are clear. Entrance fees vary based on the specific area and activity, ranging from 1,000 to 3,000 LKR (approximately 5 to 15 USD) for foreigners.

Transportation options to the site include buses, trains, taxis, or the iconic tuk-tuk, with convenient connections from nearby towns like Nuwara Eliya, Hatton, or Kandy.

Explore beyond these mentioned UNESCO World Heritage Sites in Sri Lanka and uncover a myriad of treasures like the ancient marvels of Anuradhapura and Polonnaruwa, the historical charm of Galle's old town fortified with rich history, the spiritual allure of Kandy's sacred city, and the pristine wonders of the Sinharaja Forest Reserve.

Each site boasts its distinct charm and captivating history, promising to evoke a sense of wonder and appreciation for Sri Lanka's breathtaking beauty and rich cultural tapestry. Don't hesitate – seize the opportunity to embark on a journey to Sri Lanka today. Book your trip and immerse yourself in the wonders that await, creating memories that will forever linger!

Chapter 3: Accommodation Options

3.1 Hotels and Resorts

Sri Lanka is an idyllic destination for those seeking a serene and luxurious escape on a tropical island. Whether your preference leans towards a cost-effective guesthouse, an opulent resort, or an option, the country offers a diverse range of accommodations tailored to your needs and desires. Below, discover some of Sri Lanka's premier hotels and resorts for your consideration.

Colombo

<u>Kindly Scan the QR Code or click on the link for accurate map directions.</u>

Colombo, the vibrant capital and largest city of Sri Lanka, is a bustling center of culture, commerce, and entertainment. As an excellent launchpad for exploring the rest of the country, Colombo provides convenient access to the airport, train station, and bus terminal. For those seeking accommodation in the heart of the city, consider the following hotels and resorts:

- **Shangri-La Hotel Colombo**: A distinguished five-star hotel, this establishment boasts breathtaking views of the Indian Ocean, Beira Lake, and the city skyline. It is situated in the popular Galle Face Green area. It offers 500 spacious rooms, suites, and amenities such as a spa, fitness center, outdoor pool, and various dining options. Close to attractions like the Gangaramaya Temple, National Museum, and Old Parliament Building, prices range from $200 to $400 per night, depending on the season and room type. Book online on [their website](https://www.shangri-la.com/en/colombo/shangrila/) or call +94 11 788 8288.

- **Cinnamon Grand Colombo:** This four-star hotel combines luxury and convenience, offering 501 rooms and suites, a spa, a gym, a pool, and an impressive array of 14 restaurants and bars. It is situated in the city's heart and close to key landmarks such as Galle Face Green, the World Trade Center, and the Colombo City Centre. Prices range from $100 to $300 per night, varying with the season and room type. Secure your reservation online via [their website] or contact them at +94 - 11 - 2161161.

- **CityRest Fort:** Catering to budget-conscious travelers, this hotel provides a snug and inviting stay with 33 rooms, a café, a lounge, and a rooftop terrace. Nestled in the Fort area, the historical and commercial heart of the city, it offers proximity to attractions like the Dutch Hospital, Pettah Market, and Colombo Fort Railway Station. Nightly rates range from $20 to $50, depending on the season and room type. Book your stay online at [Booking.com]

Kandy

For Accurate Map Direction, click on the link or Scan the QR Code

Kandy, the second-largest city in Sri Lanka and the country's cultural and spiritual capital, holds the prestigious title of a UNESCO World Heritage Site. This designation is owing to its hosting of the Temple of the Sacred Tooth Relic, the revered Buddhist shrine in Sri Lanka. For those seeking accommodation in this charming and historically rich city, consider the following hotels and resorts:

- **Earl's Regency:** A five-star establishment offering a picturesque vista of the Mahaweli River and the surrounding mountains. It promises a luxurious stay with 104 rooms and suites, a spa, a fitness center, a pool, and three restaurants. Situated on the outskirts, approximately 5 km from the Temple of the Sacred Tooth Relic, Kandy Lake, and the Royal Botanical Gardens. Prices range from $150 to $350 per night, contingent on the season and room type. Secure your booking through [Booking.com].

- **OZO Kandy:** A four-star hotel offering a contemporary and chic experience. It provides a modern stay with 122 rooms, a gym, a pool, and two dining options. Situated in the city center, approximately 2 km from the Temple of the Sacred Tooth Relic, Kandy Lake, and the Kandy City Centre. Prices range from $80 to $200 per night, contingent on the season and room type. Secure your booking through [this website]

- **Clock Inn Kandy:** A budget-friendly hotel offering a vibrant and comfortable stay. With ten rooms, a café, a lounge, and a garden, it ensures an affordable yet pleasant experience. Located in the city center, approximately 1 km from the Temple of the Sacred Tooth Relic, Kandy Lake, and the Kandy Railway Station. Prices range from $15 to $40 per night, contingent on the season and room type. Secure your booking through [their website] or by calling them at +94 81 222 2888.

3.2 Guest Houses and B&Bs

If you seek a more intimate and genuine experience in Sri Lanka, opting for a guest house or bed and breakfast (B&B) presents an excellent choice. Immerse yourself in the warmth of local hosts who can provide valuable insights and tips about the culture and attractions of the region. Indulge in the flavors of authentic, home-cooked Sri Lankan cuisine, a culinary journey that varies across different regions. Guest houses and B&Bs, widely available throughout the country, offer a cost-effective alternative to hotels, catering to every corner, from vibrant urban centers to the tranquil countryside.

Here are some of the best guest houses and B&Bs in Sri Lanka that you can book for your 2024 trip:

Scan the QR Code or Click on the Link for Map Directions

Galle: Positioned on the southern coast of Sri Lanka, Galle is a historic port city renowned for its impeccably preserved

Dutch fort, a UNESCO World Heritage Site. Embracing beach enthusiasts, Galle boasts numerous stunning beaches and resorts nearby. Should you desire accommodation within the old town, consider Fort Bazaar, an elegant and contemporary Bed and Breakfast in a 17th-century merchant's house. Prices range from $150 to $250 per night, contingent on the season and room type. Contact them at +94 773 638 381 or visit their website [www.teardrop-hotels.com/fort-bazaar].

Nuwara Eliya: Nestled in the central highlands of Sri Lanka, Nuwara Eliya stands as a charming hill station celebrated for its refreshing climate, picturesque landscapes, and the enduring charm of its British colonial legacy. As the primary tea-producing region in the country, visitors can explore tea factories and plantations, gaining insights into the production process while savoring a variety of tea blends. For a snug and traditional Bed and Breakfast experience, consider [The Hill Club], a historic establishment founded in 1876 as a gentlemen's club. Prices range from $40 to $60 per night, contingent on the season and room type. Contact them at +94522222883.

These represent just a selection of the numerous guest houses and B&Bs scattered across Sri Lanka. Additional options can be explored on platforms like

[Expedia] or [Tripadvisor]. Opting to stay in a guest house or B&B offers a unique opportunity to engage with the warm and welcoming Sri Lankan locals, immersing oneself in their vibrant and diverse culture. Your time in this exquisite island nation will be filled with memorable and delightful experiences.

3.3 Eco-Lodges and Camping

Suppose you seek a more daring and environmentally conscious way to immerse yourself in the natural wonders of Sri Lanka. In that case, you may consider lodging at an eco-lodge or camping site. These choices offer a heightened connection to the environment, minimizing your ecological footprint while contributing to local communities. In this segment, we'll introduce you to some of Sri Lanka's finest eco-lodges and camping sites, providing an opportunity for a pleasant and unforgettable stay.

What are Eco-Lodges and Camping Sites?

Eco-lodges and camping sites represent sustainable and environmentally conscious forms of accommodation. They typically harness renewable energy sources like solar or wind power and implement waste recycling or composting practices. The primary goal is to uphold the integrity of the natural environment and biodiversity, often involving the active engagement of local communities.

Eco-lodges, characterized by their small-scale and low-impact designs, provide snug and rustic rooms or cabins that seamlessly integrate with the surrounding landscape. These establishments often feature communal spaces, such as lounges, dining areas, or gardens, fostering opportunities for socialization and relaxation. Many eco-lodges also curate experiences like guided tours, yoga sessions, or cooking classes, showcasing the local culture and nature.

On the other hand, camping sites adopt an open-air and uncomplicated approach, offering tents or huts that provide essential shelter and amenities. Shared bathrooms, kitchens, or fire pits encourage guests to cook and socialize. Some camping sites may even provide rental options for equipment such as sleeping bags, mattresses, or lanterns, enhancing the overall camping experience.

Why Stay at an Eco-Lodge or Camping Site?

Opting for an eco-lodge or camping site presents numerous advantages, benefiting you and the environment. Here are compelling reasons to consider this accommodation choice:

- **Environmental Impact:** Embracing this option reduces your carbon footprint and minimizes environmental impact. Utilizing fewer energy resources, conserving water, and reducing waste and pollution contribute to sustainable practices.

- **Local Support:** Choosing locally owned and operated establishments aids the local economy and community. Purchasing local products and services becomes a tangible way to support the region.

- **Cultural and Natural Exploration:** Engaging with hosts and guides and participating in offered activities enriches your understanding of local culture and nature. It provides an immersive experience that goes beyond conventional tourist encounters.

- **Authentic Immersion:** Proximity to nature fosters a more authentic and immersive experience. Witnessing wildlife and scenery firsthand enhances the overall connection with the surroundings.

- **Adventure and Enjoyment:** Venturing off the beaten path and trying new and unique activities inject fun and adventure into your travel experience. This approach encourages a more dynamic and enjoyable journey.

Where to Stay at an Eco-Lodge or Camping Site?

Sri Lanka boasts an array of eco-lodges and camping sites spread across diverse regions, catering to various budgets and preferences. Discover some standout options based on web search results:

Kindly Scan the QR code or click on the link for accurate map directions.

Back of Beyond - Wild Haven:

Description: A pocket-friendly and family-oriented eco lodge near Yala National Park. Stay in spacious cottages crafted from natural materials and powered by solar energy. Enjoy safari tours, birdwatching, and hiking, complemented by home-cooked meals.

Website: [Back of Beyond - Wild Haven](website link)

Aarunya Nature Resort and Spa:

Description: A luxurious and romantic eco-lodge atop the Kandy Mountain Range. Revel in elegant villas featuring private infinity pools and panoramic valley views. Indulge in spa services, yoga classes, and gourmet cuisine.

Website: [Aarunya Nature Resort and Spa](https://www.aarunyaresort.com/)

Cinnamon Wild Yala:

Description: A wild and exotic eco-lodge bordering Yala National Park. Experience rustic chalets overlooking the jungle or lake, jeep safaris, wildlife observation, cultural tours, and a rooftop bar.

Website: [Cinnamon Wild Yala](https://www.cinnamonhotels.com/cinnamonwildyala)

Back of Beyond - Dune Camp:

Description: A fun and laid-back camping site on Kirinda Beach. Stylish tents with private bathrooms and verandas offer surfing, snorkeling, fishing, barbecue nights, and bonfires.

Website: [Back of Beyond - Dune Camp](https://www.backofbeyond.lk/locations/yala-dune-camp.html)

Banyan Lodge Yala:

Description: A charming and intimate eco-lodge near Yala National Park. Simple and clean rooms with private bathrooms and garden views, coupled with safari tours, bicycle rental, and shared communal spaces.

Website: [Banyan Lodge Yala]

Lime & Co Kaba:

Description: A modern and minimalist eco-lodge near Mirissa Beach. Bright rooms with private bathrooms and balconies featuring shared amenities like a kitchen, swimming pool, terrace, and complimentary Wi-Fi.

Website: [Lime & Co Kaba]

Madulkelle Tea and Eco Lodge:

Description: A scenic and serene eco-lodge in the Knuckles Mountain Range. Luxurious tents with private bathrooms, a heated pool, a library, a games room, tea plantation tours, hiking, and cycling.

Website: [Madulkelle Tea and Eco Lodge]

Polwaththa Eco Lodge:

A cozy and authentic eco-lodge in the Kandy Forest. Wooden and mud cabins with private bathrooms and forest views offer yoga classes, meditation sessions, massage treatments, and organic vegetarian cuisine.

Website: [Polwaththa Eco Lodge]

The Rainforest Eco Lodge:

Description: A stunning and secluded eco-lodge in the Sinharaja Rainforest. Eco-friendly chalets with private bathrooms and rainforest views provide guided walks, birdwatching, butterfly spotting, a souvenir shop, and a restaurant.

Website: [The Rainforest Eco Lodge]

The Backwaters Lodge:

Description: A peaceful and rustic eco-lodge near Wilpattu National Park. Traditional huts with private bathrooms and lake views offer safari tours, canoeing, fishing, campfires, and barbecues.

Website: [The Backwaters Lodge](https://backwaterslodge.com/)

Kalundewa Retreat:

A tranquil and elegant eco-lodge in the Dambulla Valley. Luxury chalets with private bathrooms and lake views featuring a swimming pool, fitness center, spa, library, and restaurant.

Website: [Kalundewa Retreat](https://www.kalundewaretreat.com/)

Kodev:

Description: A unique and adventurous camping site on Kalpitiya Lagoon. Dome-shaped, waterproof tents with private bathrooms and lagoon views. Activities include kite surfing, dolphin watching, island hopping, a bar, and a restaurant.

Website: [Kodev](https://www.kodev.lk/)

Yala Safari Camping:

Description: A thrilling camping site in the heart of Yala National Park. Comfortable tents with private bathrooms and safari views, offering jeep safaris, wildlife photography, cultural shows, buffets, and a bar.

Website: [Yala Safari Camping](https://srilankayalasafari.com/)

Tri by Amaya:

Description: A chic and sophisticated eco-lodge on the banks of Koggala Lake. Stylish suites with private bathrooms and lake views boast a rooftop pool, yoga studio, spa, library, and restaurant.

Website: [Tri by Amaya](https://www.boutiquecollectionbyamaya.com/tri-koggala/)

Explore these distinctive eco-lodges and camping sites for a truly enriching experience in Sri Lanka.

How do you book an Eco-Lodge or Camping Site?

Booking an eco-lodge or camping site in Sri Lanka is easy and convenient, thanks to the various online platforms and websites that offer this service. You can browse the different options, compare the prices and features, read the reviews and ratings, and make your reservation online. Some of the best websites to book an eco-lodge or camping site in Sri Lanka are:

This is one of the most popular and reliable websites for booking accommodation worldwide, including eco-lodges and camping sites in Sri Lanka. It offers many options, from budget to luxury and urban to rural. It also offers free cancellation, customer support, and loyalty rewards.

This is another well-known and trusted website for booking accommodation worldwide, including eco-lodges and camping sites in Sri Lanka. It offers a similar range of options as Booking.com, sometimes with lower prices and better deals. It also offers free cancellation, customer support, and loyalty rewards.

This is a specialized website for booking eco-friendly accommodation worldwide, including eco-lodges and camping sites in Sri Lanka. It offers a curated selection of options, from budget to luxury and urban to rural. It also offers free cancellation, customer support, and eco-certification.

Tips and Advice for Staying at an Eco-Lodge or Camping Site

Embarking on a stay at an eco-lodge or camping site in Sri Lanka is a truly enriching experience, but proper preparation and awareness are key. To enhance your Journey, consider the following tips:

1. Pack Wisely for the Journey: Light and practical packing is crucial in remote areas, where eco-lodges and camping sites are often situated. Minimize your luggage to essentials, considering potential long walks or reliance on public transportation. Pack weather-appropriate clothing, including a hat, sunglasses, sunscreen, insect repellent, raincoat, flashlight, and a reusable water bottle. Check with your accommodation regarding provided amenities or equipment such as towels, bedding, toiletries, or bicycles.

2. Respect the Environment and Local Community: Recognize that staying in such accommodations involves sharing resources with the environment and the local community. Be mindful of your impact by adhering to accommodation rules. Conserve water and electricity, dispose of waste responsibly, opt for biodegradable or organic products, and avoid causing noise disruptions or disturbing wildlife. Respect local customs, seek permission before taking photos or entering private premises, and foster a harmonious relationship with the community.

3. Embrace the Adventure: Your stay at an eco-lodge or camping site presents a unique opportunity to immerse yourself in the natural beauty and tranquility of Sri Lanka. Embrace the adventure by exploring the surroundings, participating in offered activities, interacting with hosts and fellow guests, and savoring local cuisine. Take time to unwind, appreciating the simplicity and joy of the experience.

Prepare for a fulfilling and respectful stay, allowing the essence of Sri Lanka's natural beauty and community spirit to enhance your Journey.

Chapter 4: Dining and Cuisine

Sri Lanka is a culinary haven for enthusiasts, boasting many dishes that mirror the island's intricate history, diverse culture, and geographical charm. Whether your palate craves zesty curries, crunchy snacks, or delectable desserts, Sri Lanka offers a culinary adventure that will surely delight you. This section will acquaint you with some of the most authentic and mouthwatering Sri Lankan dishes that should be on your must-try list.

4.1 Authentic Sri Lankan Culinary Delights

Various influences, including the abundance of local ingredients, climatic conditions, religious practices, and the lasting impact of colonial history, shape the gastronomic landscape of Sri Lanka. Fundamental elements in Sri Lankan cuisine are rice, coconut, and an array of spices, harmoniously blended to craft diverse dishes that showcase regional nuances. Below, we present some of the quintessential and time-honored Sri Lankan delicacies that warrant exploration:

Rice and Curry: This dish represents the culinary essence of Sri Lanka, serving as a staple for many. Known as rice and curry, it features a generous portion of steamed rice and an array of small bowls containing various curries like chicken, fish, beef, or vegetables. The curries typically carry a bit of spice, but you can request milder options. Among the common curries are dal (lentil curry), polos (jackfruit curry), parippu (pumpkin curry), and beetroot curry. Complementing these flavors are side dishes such as pol sambal (coconut relish), lung iris (onion and chili paste), and papadum (crispy flatbread). Available in most dining establishments, rice and curry are priced between 200 and 500 LKR ($1 to $2.5), varying based on quality and quantity.

Kottu: Kottu, a popular street food originating in the northern Sri Lankan Tamil community, has now gained widespread popularity nationwide. The preparation involves chopping roti (flatbread) with two metal blades on a hot grill and mixing it with various vegetables, eggs, cheese, and meat. The result is a delectable and satisfying dish that allows for customization according to personal preferences. Varieties include chicken, beef, mutton, seafood kottu, or a vegetarian option. Typically served with a spicy gravy or curry sauce and occasionally topped with a fried egg, kottu is best savored during the evening, accompanied by the distinctive sounds of clanging blades and the enticing aroma of frying roti. Kottu stalls are prevalent in most towns and cities, with prices ranging from 300 to 600 LKR ($1.5 to $3), depending on the chosen ingredients and size.

Hoppers: Hoppers, a delectable Sri Lankan dish, are pancakes crafted from a batter comprising rice flour, coconut milk, and yeast, cooked in a distinctive small round pan. There are two primary variants: plain hoppers and egg hoppers. The former are thin and crispy with a soft, fluffy center, while the latter incorporate a fried egg in the middle. Typically enjoyed for breakfast or as a snack, hoppers come with an array of toppings such as seeni sambol (caramelized onion relish), katta sambol (dried fish and chili paste), or jaggery (palm sugar). Occasionally, hoppers are filled with chicken, fish, or potato curries. Easily accessible in hotels, guesthouses, street stalls, and cafes, hoppers' prices vary from 50 to 200 LKR ($0.25 to $1), depending on the type and quantity.

4.2 Street Food and Snacks

Sri Lanka is a haven for gastronomic delights enthusiasts, particularly those with a penchant for street food and snacks. This tropical paradise boasts a culinary tapestry that mirrors its vibrant culture, storied history, and diverse geography. From zesty and savory to delightful and crisp, Sri Lanka offers many options to tantalize every palate. Below, we present some of the finest street food and snacks that beckon exploration on your upcoming Journey through this captivating island destination.

Lamprais: Originating from the Dutch Burgher community in Sri Lanka, Lamprais is a distinctive and flavorful dish that features rice cooked with an array of meats, spices, and stock. This delectable creation is then carefully wrapped in a banana leaf and an assortment of side dishes. These may include boiled eggs, fried plantains, seeni sambol (caramelized onion relish), and cutlets (fried fish or meatballs). A banana leaf imparts a fragrant aroma and taste to the rice and its accompanying delights, ensuring a delightful and fulfilling culinary experience. Lamprais is typically available in bakeries or specialty shops, with prices ranging from 500 to 800 LKR ($2.5-$4) per packet.

Idiyappam: Idiyappam, a light and delicate dish, features rice flour noodles steamed to perfection and served with various accompaniments. While commonly enjoyed as a breakfast item, it can also serve as a delightful snack or a light meal. The versatility of idiyappam allows for various serving options – pairing it with coconut milk and sugar for a sweet indulgence or combining it with curry and sambol (spicy coconut relish) for a savory experience. Additionally, idiyappam is available in different flavors and colors, including red (beetroot), green (pandan), or yellow (turmeric). Widely accessible in restaurants, cafes, and street stalls, an idiyappam plate typically costs around 100-200 LKR ($0.5-$1).

Watalappam: Watalappam, a luscious and decadent dessert, is crafted from a blend of coconut milk, eggs, jaggery (unrefined sugar), and a medley of spices like cardamom, cinnamon, and nutmeg. Originating as a traditional Muslim dish, Watalappam has transcended cultural boundaries, delighting individuals of various backgrounds and religions. It has a velvety and custard-like consistency and boasts a sweet and spicy flavor profile. Typically served chilled and adorned with cashew nuts or raisins, Watalappam can be savored in restaurants, bakeries, or street stalls, with a slice costing around 100-200 LKR ($0.5-$1).

Short eats: These bite-sized snacks offer a quick and flavorful indulgence, commonly found in bakeries, cafes, or street stalls, boasting various shapes, sizes, and flavors. Among the most prevalent short eats are:

- **Cutlets:** Fried spheres of fish or meat blended with potatoes, onions, and spices, encased in a crispy exterior and a tender interior. Often accompanied by chili or tomato sauce.

- **Samosas:** Triangular pastries filled with spiced potatoes, peas, onions, and occasionally meat. Deep-fried to a golden and crunchy perfection, usually enjoyed with mint chutney or ketchup.

- **Patties:** Flaky pastries filled with meat, fish, or vegetables, baked to a golden and crisp finish. Resembling empanadas or pies, they are commonly paired with chili or mustard sauce.

- **Rolls:** Similar to spring rolls but with a thicker and softer wrapper, these are filled with meat, fish, or vegetables and deep-fried until golden and crisp. Often served with chili sauce or vinegar sauce.

- **Buns**: Soft and fluffy bread filled with meat, fish, cheese, or jam, baked until golden and soft. Typically enjoyed with butter or margarine.

- **Cakes:** Sweet and moist cakes crafted from semolina, coconut, dates, or fruits. They pair well with tea or coffee and are topped with icing, nuts, or dried fruits.

- **Cookies:** Crunchy buttery cookies featuring ingredients such as cashew nuts, sesame seeds, or chocolate chips. Often flavored with vanilla, cardamom, or cinnamon, these are best enjoyed with tea or coffee.

These delectable treats, costing around 50-100 LKR ($0.25-$0.5) each, complement a hot or cold beverage. Sri Lanka, a haven for street food enthusiasts, offers many options for hearty meals, light snacks, or sweet indulgences. Embark on a culinary journey through the vibrant streets of Sri Lanka to uncover the flavors and stories behind each dish, promising an unforgettable experience!

Chapter 5: Things to Do and Outdoor Activities

5.1 Beach Activities

Sri Lanka has over 1,300 km of coastline, offering various beach activities for all travelers. Whether looking for relaxation, adventure, culture, or wildlife, you will find something to suit your taste and budget on the island's stunning beaches. In this chapter, we will introduce you to some of the best beach activities in Sri Lanka that you can enjoy in 2024.

Surfing

Adorned with over 1,300 km of coastline, Sri Lanka presents many beach activities catering to diverse preferences and budgets. Whether seeking relaxation, adventure, cultural exploration, or wildlife encounters, the island's breathtaking beaches offer an array of experiences in 2024. Here, we introduce you to some of the finest beach activities.

Sri Lanka emerges as a haven for surf enthusiasts, boasting consistent waves, warm waters, and diverse breaks suitable for surfers of all skill levels. The optimal surfing periods are from October to April along the south and west coasts and from May to September on the east coast. Explore some of the most renowned surfing spots:

Scan the QR Code or Click on the link for Accurate Maps

- **Arugam Bay:** Recognized as the surf capital of Sri Lanka, Arugam Bay, situated on the east coast, beckons with its long and consistent right-hand point break, yielding waves reaching up to 5 meters. Ideal for intermediate to advanced surfers, the bay offers a laid-back ambiance with numerous surf shops, cafes, bars, and accommodation options. Notable nearby breaks include Whiskey Point, Peanut Farm, and Pottuvil Point, catering to varying skill levels. Surfboard rentals are available at around 1,000 LKR (5 USD) daily, with surf lessons offered at approximately 2,500 LKR (13 USD) per hour. Arugam Bay Surf is a reputable surf school providing lessons, rentals, and tours.

- **Hikkaduwa:** Positioned on the southwest coast, Hikkaduwa stands as one of Sri Lanka's oldest and most beloved surf destinations. Boasting a range of breaks, from gentle beach breaks to powerful reef breaks, it accommodates surfers from beginners to experts. The primary surf season spans from November to March, with robust and consistent waves. Main Reef, a fast and hollow left-hander breaking over a coral reef, is a renowned break suitable for advanced surfers seeking thrilling rides with barrels and aerials. Additional breaks in Hikkaduwa include Beach Break, Inside Reef, and Benny's. Hikkaduwa exudes a vibrant atmosphere with numerous surf shops, restaurants, nightclubs, and hotels. Surfboard rentals are approximately 800 LKR (4 USD) daily, and surf lessons cost around 2,000 LKR (10 USD) per hour. [Hikkaduwa Surf School] is a reliable option for lessons, rentals, and camps.

Embark on a surfing adventure along Sri Lanka's picturesque coasts, where the waves tell stories and the beaches invite you to discover the thrill of the ocean.

Snorkeling and Diving

Sri Lanka is an exceptional destination for snorkeling and diving, featuring a diverse marine ecosystem, vibrant coral reefs, intriguing shipwrecks, and hidden underwater caves. The prime time for these aquatic adventures is from October to April along the South and west coasts, while the east coast offers optimal conditions from May to September. Let's explore some of the premier snorkeling and diving spots in Sri Lanka:

Pigeon Island: Nestled off the coast of Nilaveli on the northeast coast, Pigeon Island is a designated national park safeguarding a pristine coral reef and serving as a nesting site for pigeons. Renowned as one of Sri Lanka's top snorkeling and diving locations, Pigeon Island offers encounters with a spectrum of colorful marine life, including fish, corals, turtles, sharks, and rays. The crystalline and tranquil waters exhibit depths ranging from 3 to 15 meters. Accessible by boat from Nilaveli, the journey costs approximately 3,000 LKR (15 USD) per person, covering the entrance fee and snorkeling gear. Alternatively, diving trips from Nilaveli can be arranged at around 10,000 LKR (50 USD) per person, including equipment and a guide. [Nilaveli Diving Centre] is a reputable diving center providing professional snorkeling and diving excursions to Pigeon Island.

Unawatuna: Positioned on the south coast near Galle, Unawatuna charms visitors with its crescent-shaped bay, sandy beaches, turquoise waters, and vibrant nightlife. Beyond its tourist appeal, Unawatuna offers splendid opportunities for snorkeling and diving, allowing exploration of coral reefs, rock formations, and intriguing shipwrecks within the bay. The warm and shallow waters present depths ranging from 5 to 25 meters. Snorkeling gear can be rented from the beach for approximately 500 LKR (2.5 USD) daily. Diving enthusiasts can book trips from Unawatuna, with costs averaging around 8,000 LKR (40 USD) per person, covering equipment and a guide. [Unawatuna Diving Centre] is a distinguished diving center offering reliable snorkeling and diving excursions in Unawatuna.

Embark on an underwater journey in Sri Lanka, where the depths reveal a mesmerizing tapestry of marine wonders, ensuring an unforgettable experience for snorkelers and divers alike.

Whale and Dolphin Watching

Sri Lanka stands as a premier destination worldwide for observing whales and dolphins, thanks to its strategic location along the migration routes of these awe-inspiring marine creatures. The optimal period to witness these majestic beings in Sri Lanka is from November to April along the South and west coasts and from May to October on the east coast. Let's explore some of the prime locations for whale and dolphin watching in Sri Lanka:

Mirissa: Nestled along the south coast, Mirissa is a quaint town renowned for its exceptional whale and dolphin-watching excursions. It stands out as one of the finest spots to encounter the magnificent blue whales, the largest creatures on our planet, alongside other species such as sperm, fin, humpback, and killer whales. Additionally, spinner, bottlenose, and Risso's dolphins often grace the waters, swimming alongside the boats. Typically commencing early in the morning, around 6:00 am, these tours extend for approximately 4 hours. The cost is approximately 6,000 LKR (30 USD) per person, covering the boat, guide, breakfast, and insurance. [Raja and the Whales] is a highly regarded company offering exceptional whale and dolphin-watching experiences from Mirissa.

Kalpitiya: On the northwest coast, Kalpitiya is renowned for its scenic lagoons, islands, and beaches. It also stands as a hotspot for whale and dolphin watching, providing opportunities to witness large dolphin pods, sometimes up to 1,000. The waters around Kalpitiya are also frequented by sperm whales, Bryde's, and dwarf sperm whales. Tours typically commence around 7:00 am and last for approximately 3 hours. The cost is around 5,000 LKR (25 USD) per person, including the boat, guide, breakfast, and insurance. [Dolphin Beach Resort] is a comfortable resort offering whale and dolphin-watching tours from Kalpitiya.

Embark on a thrilling adventure in Sri Lanka's coastal waters, where the tales of these incredible marine creatures unfold, creating memories that linger as a testament to nature's wonders.

5.2 Wildlife and Nature Tours

Sri Lanka stands as an idyllic haven for wildlife and nature enthusiasts, offering an array of tours and activities that bring you up close to the island's extraordinary flora and fauna. Whether your fascination lies with elephants, leopards, birds, whales, or turtles, there's a curated tour for every nature lover. Delve into some of the most captivating wildlife and nature tours awaiting you in Sri Lanka:

Elephant Encounter Exclusive Tour 2024: Tailored for those seeking a personal rendezvous with Sri Lanka's gentle giants, this tour takes you to the Pinnawala Elephant Orphanage. Here, you can engage in feeding, bathing, and playful interactions with orphaned and injured elephants. The journey continues to the Millennium Elephant Foundation, providing insights into elephant conservation and welfare, with an optional opportunity to ride one. Lastly, explore the Kaudulla National Park, home to Asia's largest gathering of wild elephants. Ideal for families and animal enthusiasts, this 7-day tour costs 660 USD per person, covering accommodation, transportation, entrance fees, and meals.

Wildlife Expedition Across Sri Lanka - 10 Days: Crafted for those eager to delve into the diverse wildlife, this 10-day tour encompasses visits to Yala National Park, renowned for leopard sightings, Udawalawe National Park with its herds of elephants, and Sinharaja Forest Reserve, a haven for endemic birds, reptiles, and insects. The adventure extends to Mirissa Beach for a thrilling whale and dolphin-watching cruise. Priced at 1,684 USD per person, the tour caters to adventure seekers and nature enthusiasts, covering accommodation, transportation, entrance fees, and meals.

Avian Discovery Expedition - 07 Days: Tailored for ardent bird enthusiasts and photographers, this 7-day tour explores Kitulgala Forest Reserve for sightings of endemic and endangered species, Sinharaja Forest Reserve for endemic birds, Bundala National Park for migratory and resident waterbirds, and Horton Plains National Park for rare avian species. Priced at 1,321 USD per person, the tour includes accommodation, transportation, entrance fees, and meals.

These highlighted tours offer merely a glimpse into the plethora of wildlife and nature experiences available in Sri Lanka. Numerous options await, allowing you to tailor your choice based on interests, budget, and time constraints. For further details and reviews, explore tour operators' websites or refer to platforms like TourRadar or TripAdvisor. Sri Lanka is a remarkable destination for wildlife and nature enthusiasts, promising an unforgettable journey.

5.3 Adventure Sports

Sri Lanka is a haven for adventure enthusiasts, offering a diverse range of exhilarating sports for those seeking an adrenaline rush. Whether your passion lies in hiking, diving, fishing, climbing, ballooning, or whale watching, the island provides ample options to satisfy your adventurous cravings. Explore some of the best adventure sports Sri Lanka has to offer:

Hiking and Trekking

Sri Lanka's landscape is adorned with trails traversing expansive mountains, lush forests, paddy fields, parks, and serene villages, presenting abundant opportunities for avid hikers and trekkers. The highlands boast virgin rainforests, sacred mountains, tea gardens, and plains teeming with rare birds and insects, offering an unforgettable walking experience complemented by mild temperatures and the warm smiles of villagers. Key destinations for hiking and trekking include:

Knuckles Mountain Range: Recognized as a UNESCO World Heritage Site, this expansive area spans 155 square kilometers and features 34 peaks ranging from 900 to 2000 meters in height. With trails of varying difficulty and duration, the Knuckles Mountain Range leads adventurers through scenic landscapes, diverse ecosystems, waterfalls, caves, and historical sites. Home to numerous endemic species, such as the purple-faced langur, dwarf lizard, and Knuckles orchid, a guided hike in this range costs around $50 per person, covering transportation, entrance fees, and meals. Bookings can be made online at [Knuckles Range Trekking](https://www.tourradar.com/i/sri-lanka-adventure) or by calling +94 77 648 1464.

Ella Rock: Standing at 1350 meters, Ella Rock offers a panoramic view of surrounding hills and valleys. The approximately 4-hour round-trip hike begins at the Ella Railway Station, guiding trekkers through tea plantations, forests, streams, and bridges, showcasing breathtaking sunrise and sunset views. Moderately challenging with steep climbs and slippery paths, a guided hike to Ella Rock costs around $20 per person, covering transportation and snacks. Bookings can be made online at [Ella Rock Hiking](https://www.srilanka.travel/adventure-sports) or by calling +94 77 971 9998.

Embark on these thrilling adventures to uncover the captivating landscapes and experiences Sri Lanka has to offer.

Diving and Snorkeling

Sri Lanka, embraced by the Indian Ocean, unfolds a mesmerizing tapestry of coral gardens, exotic marine life, and ancient shipwrecks, creating an unparalleled diving and snorkeling haven. Renowned as one of the world's best destinations for underwater exploration, the southern coasts boast vibrant coral gardens, while the Galle Harbor and the Little and Great Basses house intriguing shipwrecks. The eastern and western coasts in Kalpitiya, Ampara, and Trincomalee offer unique opportunities for wreck diving, skin diving, and enchanting dolphin encounters. Explore the following popular diving and snorkeling spots in Sri Lanka:

- **Unawatuna:** Nestled on the southern coast, Unawatuna is captivating with its golden sandy beaches and turquoise waters. A diverse array of dive sites caters to varying experience levels and interests, from shallow coral reefs to deep rocky walls. The Rangoon Wreck, a British steamer sunk in 1863, rests at a depth of 30 meters and stands as Unawatuna's most renowned dive site. Adorned with corals and sponges, the wreck attracts a thriving marine ecosystem featuring barracudas, groupers, snappers, and moray eels. Dive enthusiasts can embark on this underwater adventure for approximately $40 per person, covering equipment, boats, and guides. Bookings can be made online at [Unawatuna Diving

Centre](https://www.rapidadventures.lk/) or by calling +94 77 791 0202.

Embark on an unforgettable journey into Sri Lanka's aquatic wonders, where each dive reveals a vibrant tapestry of marine life and submerged history.

Chapter 6: Art, Culture, and Entertainment

6.1 Traditional Music and Dance

Sri Lanka boasts a vibrant and diverse musical and dance heritage shaped by various ethnicities, religions, and historical epochs. The island has numerous traditional music and dance forms, each distinguished by its unique style, instruments, attire, and rituals. Some of the widely embraced and practiced traditions include:

Kandyan Dance: Kandyan dance, the classical art of the Sinhalese people, originates from the hill capital of Kandy. It features dynamic movements, intricate footwork, and elaborate costumes and masks. Accompanied by drums, flutes, and cymbals, the dancers portray tales from Buddhist mythology and folklore. The three main types are Ves, Naiyandi, and Uda Rata. Catch an awe-inspiring Kandyan dance show at the Kandy Lake Club, with daily performances at 5:30 pm for $10 per person. For reservations, contact +94 81 222 1697 or visit www.kandylakeclub.com.

Low Country Dance: Low country dance, prevalent in the southern and western coastal regions, reflects influences from Portuguese and Dutch colonial cultures. Marked by graceful movements and vibrant costumes, the dance unfolds narratives of demons, spirits, and exorcisms. Drums, tambourines, and rattles provide the musical backdrop. The four main types are Raksha, Sanni, Kolam, and Maru. Witness the enchanting spectacle at the Galle Fort Cultural Centre, hosting daily shows at 6:00 pm for $8 per person. Reach out to +94 91 222 2858 or visit www.gallefortculturalcentre.com.

Bharatanatyam Dance: Bharatanatyam, the classical dance of the Tamil people, originated in South Indian temples. Characterized by expressive gestures, intricate poses, and rhythmic footwork, it unfolds stories from Hindu mythology and literature. The two main styles are Kalakshetra and Vazhuvoor. Immerse yourself in the beauty of Bharatanatyam at the Jaffna Cultural Centre, with free weekly performances on Saturdays at 7:00 pm. Contact +94 21 222 1459 or visit www.jaffnaculturalcentre.com.

These represent just a glimpse of the rich tapestry of traditional music and dance in Sri Lanka. Explore [Rhythms of Paradise] or [YouTube] for more options. Attending a traditional performance promises an opportunity to embrace Sri Lankan culture's beauty and diversity, immersing yourself in the passion and joy of the performers for an unforgettable experience.

6.2 Art Galleries and Museums

Steeped in art, culture, and history, Sri Lanka beckons exploration through its diverse art galleries and museums. These spaces serve as custodians, showcasing and preserving myriad artistic expressions, from ancient sculptures and paintings to contemporary artworks and traditional crafts. For an enriching and educational journey, let's explore some of the country's most captivating art galleries and museums.

Understanding Art Galleries and Museums:

Art galleries and museums are havens that curate, conserve, and celebrate various forms of art and culture. These spaces house collections ranging from artworks and artifacts to specimens, often centered around specific themes, periods, or regions. They play host to exhibitions, events, and programs that illuminate the narratives of local and international artists, unraveling the stories and histories embedded within their creations.

These institutions vary in nature – public or private, large or intimate, free or ticketed. They inhabit urban or rural landscapes, and their structures can range from historical to modern architectural marvels. Factors like design, layout, and lighting influence the ambiance within.

Why Explore Art Galleries and Museums:

Embarking on a journey through art galleries and museums offers a multitude of advantages, both personal and societal:

Cultural Insight: Gain profound insights into the art, culture, and history of Sri Lanka and beyond. Explore the representations of these narratives through artworks and artifacts, fostering a deeper comprehension of their contextual, meaningful, and significant aspects.

Aesthetic Appreciation: Immerse yourself in the beauty and creativity encapsulated in the artworks. Appreciate the skills and talents of artists, uncover new styles, genres, and techniques, and broaden your horizons.

Expression and Engagement: Express your opinions and emotions, sharing thoughts and experiences with fellow visitors, guides, and staff. Engage in discussions, debates, and idea exchanges to enrich your understanding.

Supporting the Arts: Contribute to the growth and sustainability of the art and culture sector. Support the local economy and community by paying entrance fees, acquiring souvenirs, or contributing to various causes. Venturing into these cultural sanctuaries promises an enriching exploration of Sri Lanka's diverse heritage and artistic expressions. Your journey through these spaces will undoubtedly be a memorable and educational experience, opening doors to a deeper understanding of the country's vibrant cultural tapestry.

Where to Visit Art Galleries and Museums?

Sri Lanka boasts a diverse array of art galleries and museums, each offering a unique glimpse into the country's rich cultural tapestry. Here are some notable ones worth exploring:

1. Colombo National Museum: Established in 1877, this museum is the largest and oldest in Sri Lanka. Its extensive collection spans from prehistoric times to the colonial era, showcasing artifacts and relics that highlight the nation's cultural and natural heritage. The museum also features a library, cafe, and gift shop.

2. Museum of Modern and Contemporary Art Sri Lanka (MMCA): A recent addition, MMCA, opened its doors in 2021. Focused on modern and contemporary history and events in Sri Lanka, as well as global trends and movements, the museum offers a curated selection of artworks. It includes a studio, library, and cafe.

3. The Galleries of Sapumal Foundation: Housed in the former residence of painter Harry Peiris, this intimate art gallery displays works from the influential 43rd Group of Sri Lankan artists in the 20th century. The space also features a garden, library, and gift shop.

4. Ranjiths Carving and Batik Museum: Operated by artist Ranjith Perera, this vibrant gallery showcases a colorful collection of batik products and wood carvings crafted by the artist and his family. The space includes a workshop, showroom, and gift shop.

5. Maritime Archeology Museum: Located in the Dutch Fort of Galle, this museum offers a captivating journey through Sri Lanka's maritime history and culture. It houses artifacts and exhibits from ancient times, as well as a library, cafe, and gift shop.

6. Indika Art Gallery: Nestled in Colombo, this cozy gallery, run by artist Indika Pathmananda, features a diverse collection of landscapes, portraits, and abstract paintings. The space includes a studio, lounge, and gift shop.

7. Number 11: Situated in the former residence of architect Geoffrey Bawa, this elegant gallery displays artworks and objects reflecting Bawa's personal taste and style. The venue includes a garden, library, and cafe.

8. Raja Museum: Found in the Temple of the Tooth complex in Kandy, this modest museum showcases paintings and sculptures by the renowned artist Raja, celebrated for his depictions of elephants and other animals. A gift shop complements the exhibits.

9. Lime & Co Kaba: A modern and minimalist gallery near Mirissa Beach, Lime & Co Kaba exhibits artworks by local and international artists using various media and techniques. The venue also includes a kitchen, pool, and terrace.

10. Madulkelle Tea and Eco Lodge: Nestled in the Knuckles Mountain Range, this serene gallery captures the essence of the area's natural beauty and rural life through artworks by local and international artists. The lodge features a pool, library, and restaurant.

Embark on a journey through these cultural havens to explore Sri Lanka's artistic diversity and heritage. Each venue promises a unique experience, contributing to a deeper understanding of the country's vibrant cultural expressions.

6.3 Festivals and Events

Immersing oneself in the vibrant tapestry of Sri Lanka's culture involves joining locals in celebrating numerous festivals and events. The country's calendar has diverse occasions that mirror its religious, ethnic, and historical richness. Whether you seek spiritual, cultural, or joyous experiences, their festival or event is tailored to your taste. Here are some of the noteworthy and exhilarating celebrations to participate in across Sri Lanka in 2024:

Sinhala and Tamil New Year: The most significant festival in Sri Lanka is observed by both the Sinhalese and Tamil communities on April 13th and 14th. It signifies the culmination of the harvest season and the commencement of a new year according to the solar calendar. This festival is a time of jubilation, gratitude, renewal, and reconciliation. During this festive period, people don new clothing, exchange gifts, visit family and friends, and engage in various games and rituals. Key elements of the celebration include the lighting of the oil lamp, the symbolic boiling of the milk pot, the anointing of the head with oil, and astrological predictions for the upcoming year. The festival is a sensory delight, with people indulging in a variety of traditional dishes such as kiribath (milk rice), kavum (oil cakes), kokis (crispy cookies), and aluwa (sweetmeats).

Vesak Poya: The most revered festival among Buddhists in Sri Lanka occurs on the full moon day of May, commemorating the significant events of the Buddha's life, including his birth, enlightenment, and passing away. This festival is a period of deep devotion, self-reflection, and acts of charity and compassion. Devotees visit temples to offer flowers and light lamps and listen to sermons. During this time, they adhere to the eight precepts, refraining from actions such as killing, stealing, lying, consuming intoxicants, engaging in sexual misconduct, eating after noon, indulging in entertainment, and acquiring luxurious items. The celebration is a vibrant display of light and color, with homes, streets, and public spaces adorned with lanterns, flags, and pandals – illustrated boards portraying the life of the Buddha. It is also a time of joy and generosity, marked by the distribution of free food, drinks, and gifts to the less fortunate.

Kandy Esala Perahera: The most dazzling festival in Sri Lanka unfolds in Kandy during July or August. This grand procession pays homage to the revered tooth relic of the Buddha, housed in the Temple of the Tooth in Kandy. It serves as a vibrant showcase of the nation's cultural and religious richness, also venerating Sri Lanka's guardian deities: Natha, Vishnu, Kataragama, and Pattini. Extending over ten days, each festival day carries a distinct theme and route. The procession boasts a multitude of participants, including dancers, drummers, musicians, acrobats, firebreathers, whip-crackers, and flag-bearers. Notably, the adorned elephants, draped in colorful costumes and jewelry, form a captivating part of the spectacle. The pinnacle of the festival is the Maha Perahera, the grand finale featuring the Maligawa Tusker—an elephant carrying the casket containing the revered tooth relic.

Colombo Aadi Vel Festival: This Hindu festival, celebrated in Colombo, the capital city of Sri Lanka, marks the triumph of Lord Murugan, the god of war, over the demon Surapadman. The month of Aadi (July or August) transforms the city into a lively and colorful spectacle as numerous devotees gather to honor Lord Murugan and seek his blessings. The festivities encompass a series of rituals, including the hoisting of the flag, the offering of milk, the piercing of the skin, and the carrying of the kavadi—a wooden structure adorned with peacock feathers, flowers, and fruits. A significant aspect of the festival is the chariot procession, where the image of Lord Murugan is transported from the Sri Kathiresan Kovil to the New Kathiresan Kovil, accompanied by music and dance.

Galle Literary Festival: This literary festival in the historic city of Galle, a UNESCO World Heritage Site, is a vibrant platform to showcase the finest in local and international literature, art, and culture. In January, the event encompasses diverse activities, including readings, discussions, workshops, performances, exhibitions, and tours. Drawing in some of the world's most distinguished writers, artists, and thinkers, the festival creates a dynamic dialogue, exchange, and inspiration space. It is a joyous celebration, highlighting the profound impact and aesthetic allure of literature, art, and culture while attracting a large and diverse audience of readers, enthusiasts, and students.

These represent just a glimpse of the diverse festivals and events awaiting you in Sri Lanka throughout 2024. The calendar is brimming with occasions that mirror the country's rich artistic, cultural, and entertainment tapestry. Engaging in these vibrant celebrations isn't just about reveling in the joy and thrill they offer; it's also an opportunity to delve deeper into understanding and appreciating the unique facets of this nation and its people.

Chapter 7: 7-Day Itinerary

7.1 Day 1-3: Colombo and Surroundings

Embark on a captivating journey through the enchanting landscapes of Sri Lanka, a small island with an immense personality. This 7-day itinerary invites you to explore the best of this diverse nation, commencing in the vibrant capital city of Colombo and its surrounding gems.

Day 1: Colombo

Colombo, the largest and most cosmopolitan city in Sri Lanka, unfolds a tapestry of contrasts—where the old meets the new, the traditional harmonizes with the modern, and the chaotic intertwines with the serene. Delve into the highlights of Colombo on your first day:

- Gangaramaya Temple: Explore one of Colombo's revered Buddhist temples, the Gangaramaya Temple, a testament to its historical significance dating back to the 19th century. A complex of diverse architectural styles, from Sri Lankan to Thai to Chinese, houses a rich collection of statues, relics, and artifacts. Admire the elephant museum and the library within its premises. The Temple welcomes visitors from 6 am to 10 pm, with an entrance fee of 300 LKR ($1.5) per person.

- Pettah Market: Immerse yourself in the vibrant heart of Colombo at Pettah Market, a bustling and colorful marketplace offering many goods, from clothing and electronics to spices and fruits. Navigate through its narrow streets, engage in spirited haggling with local vendors, and absorb the lively atmosphere. The market operates from 8 am to 6 pm, with no entrance fee.

- Galle Face Green: Unwind at Galle Face Green, a spacious coastal expanse in Colombo. Bask in the refreshing sea breeze, catch a breathtaking sunset, fly a kite, or indulge in local street delicacies like kottu roti, isso wade, and achcharu. The green welcomes visitors from 6 am to 9 pm, with no entrance fee.

Day 2: Kandy

Kandy, nestled in the central highlands, stands as the cultural and spiritual heart of Sri Lanka. Renowned for its sacred Temple, scenic lake, and rich historical heritage, the journey from Colombo to Kandy by train unfolds a mesmerizing panorama of lush green hills, tea plantations, and cascading waterfalls. The three-hour ride, costing approximately 500 LKR ($2.5) for a second-class ticket, offers one of Sri Lanka's most scenic and delightful experiences.

Highlights of Kandy:

- Temple of the Tooth: Immerse yourself in the holiest site in Sri Lanka, the Temple of the Tooth, where the revered relic of Buddha's tooth is enshrined. A masterpiece of Sri Lankan architecture adorned with intricate carvings, paintings, and decorations, the Temple hosts daily ceremonies and rituals. Explore the museum and library within its premises. Open from 5:30 am to 8 pm, the entrance fee is 1500 LKR ($7.5) per person.

- Kandy Lake: Stroll along the shores of the picturesque Kandy Lake, a man-made gem crafted by the last king of Kandy in the 19th century. Enjoy a leisurely walk, a serene boat ride, or a bike excursion. Admire the island at the lake's center, once the king's private harem. Open from 6 am to 6 pm, there is no entrance fee.

- Royal Botanical Gardens: Delight in the vastness and beauty of one of Sri Lanka's largest botanical gardens, sprawling across 147 acres. Home to over 4000 plant species, including orchids, palms, spices, and medicinal herbs, the gardens showcase unique attractions like the giant bamboo, cannonball tree, and the majestic avenue of royal palms. Open from 7:30 am to 5 pm, the entrance fee is 2000 LKR ($10) per person.

Day 3: Nuwara Eliya

Nuwara Eliya, a delightful town in the hill country of Sri Lanka, captivates visitors with its cool climate, colonial allure, and tea-centric culture. As the gateway to Horton Plains National Park, renowned for the breathtaking views of World's End and Baker's Falls, Nuwara Eliya is accessible by a roughly 2-hour bus ride from Kandy, costing around 200 LKR ($1) per person. Embark on a journey through the following highlights on your third day:

- Tea Factory and Plantation: Explore the heart of Sri Lanka's tea industry by visiting a tea factory and plantation in Nuwara Eliya. Immerse yourself in the history and intricate process of tea production, savoring some of the world's finest teas. Consider purchasing tea as a memorable souvenir or gift. Nuwara Eliya boasts several tea factories and plantations, including Pedro, Blue Field, and Mackwoods. Entrance fees range from 500 to 1000 LKR ($2.5 to $5) per person.

- Gregory Lake: A product of British governance in the 19th century, Gregory Lake stands as another scenic man-made lake in Nuwara Eliya. A popular recreational spot, the lake offers activities such as boating, jet skiing, horse riding, and cycling. Take in the serene views of the lake and surrounding mountains. Gregory Lake has no entrance fee and is open from 6 am to 6 pm.

- Horton Plains National Park: Delve into the UNESCO World Heritage Site of Horton Plains National Park, covering 3160 hectares of diverse landscapes, including grasslands, forests, waterfalls, and cliffs. Embark on a 9 km circular trail, a 3-hour hike that unveils key attractions like the awe-inspiring World's End, an 870-meter sheer drop, Baker's Falls, a 20-meter-high waterfall, and the majestic Sambar deer, the largest deer species in Sri Lanka. The park welcomes visitors from 6 am to 6 pm, with an entrance fee of 4000 LKR ($20) per person.

Day 3 unfolds a tapestry of tea culture, scenic beauty, and natural wonders in the enchanting town of Nuwara Eliya.

7.2 Day 4-5: Kandy and the Hill Country

After exploring the ancient marvels of Sigiriya and Dambulla, it's time to journey to the cultural heart of Sri Lanka: Kandy. Nestled amidst hills, this charming city blends history, culture, and nature. Devote two days to unraveling the beauty of Kandy and its surrounding hill country, embracing scenic vistas, vibrant temples, and a refreshing climate.

Day 4: Kandy

Commence Your Day at the Temple of the Tooth: Embark on your day by immersing yourself in the Temple of the Tooth spiritual aura, a revered site for Buddhists in Sri Lanka. Housing a relic believed to be Buddha's tooth, brought from India in the 4th century, the Temple is a masterpiece of Sri Lankan architecture. Witness daily ceremonies and rituals, exploring nearby attractions like Kandy Lake, the Royal Palace, and the National Museum. The Temple of the Tooth opens its doors to pilgrims and tourists from 5:30 am to 8 pm, with a foreigner's entrance fee of 1,500 LKR ($7.5). Kandy, situated approximately 120 km away from Colombo, is accessible by train, bus, or taxi.

Stroll Around Kandy Lake: Following your visit to the Temple of the Tooth, stroll around Kandy Lake. Crafted by the last king of Kandy in the 19th century, this man-made lake exudes serenity. Enjoy the city and hill views, take a boat ride, or explore the island in the middle, once a royal summer retreat.

Afternoon Delight at Peradeniya Botanic Gardens: Spend your afternoon at the expansive and enchanting Peradeniya Botanic Gardens, the largest in Sri Lanka. Encompassing 147 acres, the gardens boast over 4,000 plant species, including orchids, palms, spices, and medicinal plants. Marvel at giant trees planted by notable visitors like Queen Elizabeth II and Yuri Gagarin. Entrance for foreigners is 2,000 LKR ($10), and the gardens welcome visitors from 7:30 am to 5 pm. Reachable from Kandy by bus, taxi, or tuk-tuk, the gardens are approximately 6 km away.

Evening Cultural Extravaganza at Kandy Lake Club: As the evening unfolds, immerse yourself in the rich tapestry of Sri Lankan culture with a Kandyan dance performance at the Kandy Lake Club. This cultural center showcases traditional dances and music, featuring captivating performances like the fire dance, mask dance, cobra dance, and more. Marvel at the skills and courage of drummers and fire walkers. The hour-long show, starting at 5 pm, provides a vibrant insight into Sri Lanka's history and legends. Foreigners can secure tickets for 1,000 LKR ($5) online or at the venue.

Day 4 in Kandy promises a delightful blend of spirituality, nature, and cultural immersion.

Day 5: The Hill Country

On your second day in Kandy, embark on an enchanting day trip to the hill country, a region adorned with verdant mountains, tea plantations, cascading waterfalls, and picturesque villages. The hill country is one of Sri Lanka's most scenic and serene destinations, offering many activities and attractions to cater to diverse traveler preferences.

Scenic Train Journey from Kandy to Ella: Revel in one of the world's most breathtaking train journeys by boarding a train from Kandy to Ella. This captivating ride spans approximately 7 hours and traverses through awe-inspiring landscapes, including the Knuckles Mountain Range, Horton Plains National Park, Ramboda Falls, and the iconic Nine Arches Bridge. Witness the mesmerizing sight of tea pickers at work while locals wave and share smiles with passing trains. The journey provides not only stunning views but also an opportunity to mingle with new acquaintances and savor the rural life of Sri Lanka. Ticket prices range from 200 to 1,500 LKR ($1 to $7.5) for foreigners, varying based on class and availability. Secure your tickets online or at the station. Explore the [official website](insert_website_link) for additional details.

Exploring Ella and Its Charm: Upon reaching Ella, dedicate the remainder of the day to exploring this small, inviting town with a laid-back and friendly ambiance. Discover numerous cafes, restaurants, and shops catering to travelers. Ella boasts local attractions like Ella Rock, Little Adam's Peak, Ravana Falls, and Ella Spice Garden. Alternatively, opt for a tuk-tuk or taxi to visit nearby gems such as Lipton's Seat, Dambatenne Tea Factory, Diyaluma Falls, and Buduruwagala Temple. With its blend of nature, adventure, and culture, Ella provides the perfect backdrop to unwind after a scenic train journey. Accommodation options in Ella cater to various budgets, ranging from budget hostels to luxurious hotels.

These highlights offer a glimpse into your Kandy and hill country itinerary, with numerous treasures awaiting discovery. Kandy and the hill country are two of Sri Lanka's most captivating and diverse regions, promising a wealth of experiences for every type of traveler. Whether your interests lie in history, culture, nature, or adventure, the beauty of these destinations awaits your exploration. Don't hesitate to book your journey to Sri Lanka today and unravel the wonders of Kandy and the hill country.

7.3 Day 6-7: Galle and the South Coast

Day 6: Galle Fort and Unawatuna

Embark on your sixth day by immersing yourself in the rich history of Galle Fort, a UNESCO World Heritage Site tracing its roots back to the 16th century. Initially constructed by the Portuguese, later expanded by the Dutch, and eventually controlled by the British, the fort is a testament to the colonial impact on Sri Lanka's architecture and heritage. Stroll along the fort walls, revel in ocean views, and meander through charming streets adorned with boutique shops, cafes, galleries, and museums. Notable highlights within the fort include the Galle Lighthouse, the Dutch Reformed Church, the National Maritime Museum, and the Historical Mansion Museum.

After exploring the fort, venture to Unawatuna, a crescent-shaped bay renowned as one of Sri Lanka's premier beach destinations. Unawatuna beckons with sandy shores, turquoise waters, vibrant nightlife, and various activities, including snorkeling, diving, surfing, and yoga. Explore nearby attractions such as the Japanese Peace Pagoda, Jungle Beach, and the Yatagala Temple. Unawatuna offers diverse accommodation options, from budget hostels to luxury resorts and many restaurants and bars serving local and international cuisine.

Day 7: Mirissa and Weligama

On your final day, visit Mirissa, a quaint town famed for whale and dolphin-watching tours. Mirissa stands as one of the world's prime spots for observing blue whales, the largest creatures on Earth, along with sperm whales, fin whales, humpback whales, and killer whales. Tours typically commence early in the morning, around 6:00 am, and last approximately 4 hours, costing around 6,000 LKR (30 USD) per person, including the boat, guide, breakfast, and insurance. Consider Raja and the Whales, a highly regarded whale and dolphin-watching company based in Mirissa.

Post-tour, unwind on the golden expanse of Mirissa Beach, bordered by palm trees and adorned with vibrant fishing boats. Engage in water sports like surfing, kayaking, or stand-up paddleboarding, or visit the picturesque Coconut Tree Hill for a breathtaking view of the bay. Mirissa offers a variety of accommodations, from cozy guesthouses to stylish villas and an array of restaurants and cafes featuring fresh seafood and vegetarian delights.

If time permits, explore Weligama, a nearby town renowned for its stilt fishermen employing a traditional and unique fishing method. Watch these fishermen balance on wooden poles in the water while catching fish with rods and lines—an extraordinary sight. Weligama is also an excellent destination for surfing, particularly for beginners, with a wide and shallow bay boasting gentle waves and soft sands. Surfboard rentals are available for around 800 LKR (4 USD) per day, or you can opt for a surf lesson priced at approximately 2,000 LKR (10 USD) per hour. The Weligama Surf School is a reputable establishment offering lessons, rentals, and camps.

Chapter 8: Practical Information and Tips

8.1 Local Customs and Etiquette

Cultural Etiquette for Visitors in Sri Lanka

As a guest in Sri Lanka, embracing and respecting local customs is essential, ensuring a harmonious experience with the gracious Sri Lankan people. Here are some insightful tips to enhance your stay and leave a positive impression:

Greetings: In Sri Lanka, the customary greeting is "Ayubowan," expressing wishes for longevity. Accompany this with a slight bow, a warm smile, and placing your palms together in front of your chest. This gesture is versatile, serving as expressions of gratitude, farewells, and apologies. When addressing elders, monks, or individuals of higher status, deepen the bow and elevate your hands. While shaking hands is acceptable, use only the right hand, as the left is considered impure. Touching or patting someone's head is discouraged, considering it sacred.

Dress Code: Given Sri Lanka's conservative culture, modest attire is crucial, particularly when visiting religious sites. Cover your shoulders and legs, remove shoes and hats, and refrain from wearing clothing featuring images of Buddha, deemed disrespectful.

Public places do not welcome beachwear, and both nudity and toplessness are legally prohibited. Minimize flashy jewelry to avoid attracting unwarranted attention or envy.

Temple Etiquette: Sri Lanka boasts numerous sacred Buddhist and Hindu temples, demanding adherence to specific etiquette. Never turn your back on a Buddha image or pose for photos with it. Avoid pointing your feet at Buddha images and anti-clockwise walks around dagobas (stupas). Speak softly and respectfully, refraining from disturbing worshippers or monks. Express appreciation by making a small donation, offering flowers, or burning incense.

Dining Etiquette: Savor the diverse and delicious Sri Lankan cuisine, and be open to experiencing local dishes. Embrace the traditional practice of eating with your fingers, using the right hand, and washing before and after meals. Avoid using the left hand to pass food or touch it. Wastefulness is considered impolite, so finish what is served on your plate. In public, refrain from consuming alcohol, especially when interacting with monks or devout Buddhists. Respect religious dietary restrictions, avoiding beef for Hindus and pork for Muslims. Acknowledge fasting and vegetarian days, abstaining from meat or fish on these occasions.

8.2 Transportation Tips

Navigating the relatively small yet diverse island of Sri Lanka poses challenges due to traffic, road conditions, and weather. Fortunately, various transportation options cater to different preferences, budgets, and destinations. Below are some of the common and convenient ways to travel in Sri Lanka:

Train: Embarking on a train journey unveils the scenic beauty of Sri Lanka at an affordable cost. The extensive train network connects major cities and attractions like Colombo, Kandy, Ella, Nuwara Eliya, Galle, and Jaffna. Class options range from first class with reserved seats and air-conditioning to third class with wooden benches. Ticket prices, varying with distance and class, generally fall between 50 and 1000 LKR. It is advisable to book in advance, especially for popular routes like Kandy to Ella.

Bus: Bus travel is an economical and widespread option covering nearly every corner of the island. Public buses operated by the Sri Lanka Transport Board (SLTB) are budget-friendly but make frequent stops. However, slightly more expensive, private buses offer a faster and more comfortable journey, sometimes with air-conditioning. Ticket prices range from 20 to 500 LKR, and tickets can be purchased on board or at the bus station. Arriving early is recommended, especially for long-distance routes.

Taxi: Opting for a taxi provides comfort and convenience but comes at a higher cost. Taxis are available in most cities and can be hailed on the street or booked through various platforms. Metered pricing is common, but some negotiation may occur. Prices typically range from 50 to 100 LKR per kilometer. Online platforms like PickMe or Uber offer a reliable and often cheaper alternative.

Tuk-tuk: Traveling by tuk-tuk adds a touch of adventure but requires caution. These three-wheeled vehicles, accommodating up to three passengers, are prevalent throughout Sri Lanka. Ideal for short distances and navigating narrow roads, tuk-tuks are known for their maneuverability. However, they lack safety features like seat belts and may be noisy. Prices range from 40 to 80 LKR per kilometer. When using a tuk-tuk, agreeing on the price and destination beforehand or opting for a metered or online service is advisable to avoid potential issues.

8.3 Useful Phrases in Sinhala

Sinhala is the official and most widely spoken language of Sri Lanka, with about 16 million native speakers. It belongs to the Indo-Aryan branch of the Indo-European language family and has its alphabet and grammar. Learning some basic Sinhala phrases can help you communicate with the locals and show respect and appreciation for their culture. Here are some useful phrases that you can use during your trip:

Greetings and Farewells

- Hello / Good day: Āyubōvan - This is a formal and respectful way of greeting someone, which means "may you live long." You can also use Halō, which is more informal and casual.
- Good morning: Subha udhāsanak
- Good evening: Subha sandhavak
- Good night: Subha rāhthriyak
- Goodbye: Gihillā hamuvemu - This is a polite and friendly way of saying goodbye, which means "let's meet again". You can also use Gihin ennam, which means "go and come".

Introductions and Small Talk

- What is your name?: Oyāgē nama mokakda?
- My name is ...: Magē nama ...

- Where are you from?: Oya kohendha?
- I'm from ...: Mama ... ven/yen
- How are you?: Kohomadha? - This is a common and informal way of asking how someone is doing. You can also use Kohomadha saepa sanīpa? or Saepa sanīpa kohomadha? which means "how are you well?".
- I'm fine: Hondhin innavā - This is a simple and positive way of answering how you are doing. You can also use Istuti mama hodin Innova, which means "thank you, I'm fine."

Politeness and Gratitude

- Please: Karunākarala - This is a polite and respectful way of asking for something or making a request.
- Thank you: Istuti - This is a simple and sincere way of expressing gratitude or appreciation. You can also use Bohoma study, which means "thank you very much."
- You're welcome: Ekata kamak na - This is a humble and modest way of responding to thank you, which means "it's nothing".
- Sorry / Excuse me: Samāvenna - This is a general and polite way of apologizing or asking for someone's attention. You can also use Avasara,

which means "permission" when addressing priests or monks.

Questions and Answers

- Do you speak English?: Oya ingreesi kathā karanavādha? - This is a useful and courteous way of asking if someone can communicate with you in English.
- I don't understand: Mata therenne næ - This is a simple and honest way of saying that you don't comprehend something. You can also use Mata obava therum ganna baha, which means "I can't understand you".
- How do you say ... in Sinhala?: ... kiyanne kohomadha? - This is a helpful and curious way of asking how to say something in Sinhala.
- How much?: Kiyeda? - This is a common and practical way of asking the price or cost of something. You can also use Kiyeda meka? which means, "How much is this?".
- Where is ...?: ... koheda? - This is a basic and essential way of asking for directions or locations of something. For example, Where is the toilet?: Vathura koheda?.

Useful Expressions

- I'm hungry: Mata bada giniyi - This is a simple and direct way of saying that you need some food.
- I want (some) water: Mata vathura onē - This is a simple and clear way of saying that you need some water. You can also use Mata vathura venavā, which means "I want water".
- I don't feel well: Mata sanīpa nǣ - This is a simple way of saying that you are sick or unwell.
- I want/need a doctor: Mata dhōsthara kenekvā onē - This is a simple and urgent way of saying that you need medical attention. You can also use Mata dhōsthara kenekvā venavā, which means "I want a doctor".
- Help me!: Mata udauw karanā! - This is a simple and desperate way of asking for assistance or rescue.
- Let's go: Yamu - This is a simple and casual way of saying you are ready to leave or move.
- Happy birthday: Suba upan dhinayak vēva! - This is a simple and cheerful way of wishing someone

Conclusion

9.1 Final Thoughts

As you reach the culmination of this Sri Lanka travel guide, we trust that the journey through its pages has been as delightful for you as it has been for us to craft. Sri Lanka, a truly remarkable country, unfolds a tapestry of experiences catering to every kind of traveler—those seeking adventure, culture, nature, or tranquil retreats.

Yet, beyond its myriad attractions, Sri Lanka stands as a nation that will capture your senses and touch your heart and soul. The warmth and hospitality of its people, the richness of its diverse heritage, and the breathtaking landscapes all contribute to an unforgettable encounter. Sri Lanka is a place that will surprise, challenge, and inspire you—an enchanting land that beckons you to fall in love with its charms.

While this guide endeavors to encompass much of what Sri Lanka offers, the essence lies in venturing beyond its pages, embracing the unknown and the unexpected. You may discover hidden treasures and forge connections with intriguing souls in the unexplored corners. Sri Lanka merits your time and attention, and we trust this guide has aided in planning your journey to extract the utmost from your visit. May it have stirred your curiosity and excitement, propelling you to embark on your Sri Lankan adventure.

As you set forth, we wish you a journey of safety, joy, and countless memorable moments. Until we meet again, thank you for choosing this Sri Lanka travel guide, and may your time in Sri Lanka be nothing short of wonderful! Safe travels!

Printed in Great Britain
by Amazon